SELF -ESTEEM and CONFIDENCE

HONOR HEAD

W
FRANKLIN WATTS
LONDON • SYDNEY

Franklin Watts
First published in Great Britain in 2017 by The Watts Publishing Group

Credits:
Series Editor: Jean Coppendale
Series Designer: Lorraine Inglis

Picture credits:
Every attempt has been made to clear copyright. Should there be any inadvertent omission please apply to the publisher for rectification.
t = top, b = bottom , l = left, r = right, m = middle
Cover: © Shutterstock/Dooder
All images listed here are © of Shutterstock and: 4 surassawadee; 6 Lemberg Vector Studio; 7 talking heads Dream Master; 8-9 background Elesey, 8 gold star Yulia Glam, 9t Helga Esteb; 10-11PODIS; 12 Kakigori Studio; 13 Marish; 15 Bakhtiar Zein; 16-17 curtains Frame Angel, 16b Javier Brosch, 17t Eric Isselee; 17b Tinseltown; 18-19 jorgen mcleman; 20 Creatarka; 21 people Julia Tim; 22 george studio, 23t Javier Brosch; 24-25 background MP–P, 24b Rasulov; 26-27 background TaLaNoVa, 26b Lorelyn Medina; 28-29 background, kampolz, birds, Mrs. Opossum.

Note to parents and teachers: Every effort has been made by the Publishers to ensure that these websites are suitable for children, that they are of the highest educational value, and that they contain no inappropriate or offensive material. However, because of the nature of the Internet, it is impossible to guarantee that the contents of these sites will not be altered. We strongly advise that Internet access is supervised by a responsible adult.

ISBN 978 1 4451 5292 9
Printed in China

MIX
Paper from
responsible sources
FSC® C104740

Franklin Watts
An imprint of
Hachette Children's Group
Part of The Watts Publishing Group
Carmelite House
50 Victoria Embankment
London EC4Y 0DZ

An Hachette UK Company
www.hachette.co.uk

www.franklinwatts.co.uk

Contents

WHAT IS SELF-ESTEEM?

We are not born with self-esteem – it is something we learn from the way our family, friends, teachers and peers treat us.

I believe in me

Self-esteem is how you see yourself and your abilities. It is the belief that you are good enough to achieve something and that you deserve to achieve it. It is being happy with who you are, faults and all. It is knowing that you may not have model good looks or be the best at science, art or playing football, but that you have other great qualities and you are proud of who you are and what you do.

Changes

Puberty and adolescence can be challenging times. This is when your body goes through physical changes and you are finding out who you are and trying to make sense of your place in the world. Friends and peers become an important part of your life. You begin to measure yourself against what you see around you: in the media, online, in school and among your friends and peers.

Low self-esteem

All this growing, changing and comparing can badly damage our self-esteem and result in a lack of self-confidence and self-belief. We might begin to believe that everyone else is better looking, stronger, cleverer and funnier than we are. We can easily begin to see ourselves as failures and not 'good enough'.

Signs of low self-esteem

Signs of low-self-esteem are under-achieving, not wanting to join in, not making friends, allowing ourselves to be the butt of jokes, saying 'yes' to things even though we don't want to do them and, worse still, thinking we are unlovable, unworthy and stupid. Low self-esteem makes us scared to try new things or things we think are too hard for us. Or we think we'll make a fool of ourselves, look silly or make stupid mistakes and our friends will laugh at us and our family will tease us. This can stop us enjoying ourselves and trying things that we might enjoy and be really good at.

The **good** news is, we can *change* our self-esteem.

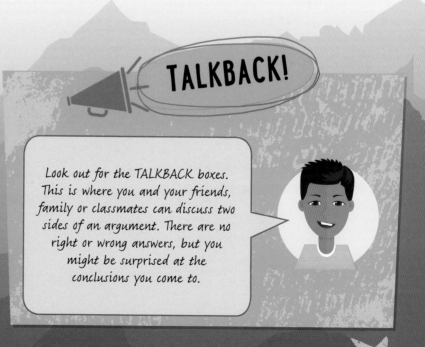

TALKBACK!

Look out for the TALKBACK boxes. This is where you and your friends, family or classmates can discuss two sides of an argument. There are no right or wrong answers, but you might be surprised at the conclusions you come to.

BODY IMAGE

Our body image is important to our self-esteem. Puberty can be a tricky time – things begin to happen to your body that can affect the way you see yourself.

Developing bodies

Between the ages of about 8 and 16, but usually around 11 to 12, young people go through puberty. Different hormones are released into your body by the brain and begin to affect the way your body looks. For girls and boys there is more hair growth on their body, girls begin to develop breasts and hips and form a womanly shape, and boys find their voices become deeper and their body shape changes as their shoulders broaden out and they develop muscles. These changes take place over several years and are perfectly natural, but we all develop differently.

Looking perfect

As children grow and change they may begin to compare themselves to their friends and media and online celebrities – singers, actors, vloggers and models. This can make girls believe that being super slim with perfect skin and glossy hair is the only way to look, or for a boy that you have to be tall, strong and athletic. We're bombarded with images of the 'ideal' way to look and can soon believe that this is the norm and if we don't look like this we're inferior.

Family influence

Some young people may begin to develop a negative body image if family members are always dieting or complaining about the way they look. If this is happening in your family talk to the person about it. Say that it's making you anxious about your own body. They may not be aware that they're being so obsessive about their looks.

TALKBACK!

Why do you think we're so obsessed by body image these days?

Fashion models and film stars make us feel fat and ugly – they always look so perfect. It's their fault.

It's not their fault, it's ours for comparing ourselves to them. They have make-up artists and hair stylists to help them look super glam.

LOVE BEING YOU!

We are all different shapes and sizes with our own features that make each one of us unique. The world would be a really boring place if we all looked the same.

Negative thoughts

If you have negative thoughts about how you look, ask why. Is it because someone made a silly remark about you months ago, or your friends tease you about something? Or maybe you assume that because of your hair colour or nose shape everyone thinks you're ugly? Or do you think people will only like you if you look glamorous and wear the latest fashions? Negative thoughts can grow until they are all you think about. You stop being able to see any positive stuff. Bad thoughts can fester away and we don't question them, just believe them as they grow out of proportion and make us feel miserable.

Be thought-wise

If your negative thoughts are stopping you doing things or enjoying yourself, you need to challenge them. Be thought-wise – if you are comparing yourself to others, ask why? How did your negative thoughts start? Did a friend say something unkind? Could it be that they're trying to hide their own insecurities? Start to think about yourself in a more positive way. Each person has something about them that is special, such as a great smile, shiny hair or beautiful hands. Remember, how we look is just a small part of who we are. Focus on what is unique about you in so many different ways and learn to love being you!

Get real!

Are your negative thoughts coming from the pictures you see in magazines and online or are you always criticising yourself? Very few people are born with amazing good looks or develop rippling muscles. Most celebrities work really hard at how they look because it's their job. They have make-up and hair experts to help them, and marketing and online photographs can be digitally retouched. This is not real life, and even the most glamorous stars have spots, bad hair days and bits about themselves they'd like to change.

How much time have I wasted on diets and what I look like? Take your time and talent and figure out what you have to contribute to this world. And get over what your butt looks like in those jeans.

America Ferrara (b. 1984), US actress

Part of growing up is accepting that there are things about yourself you cannot change. They are part of what makes you who you are.

How you treat people is far more important than how you look.

I'd rather have a friend who is kind and supportive than one who thinks about how they look all the time.

Worrying about things you can't change is boring and a waste of time.

I like being with people who can have a good laugh.

A healthy body image

Creating a healthy body image can be fun and will make you feel happier and increase your self-confidence.

Get fit!

The first way to improve your body image is to start thinking about it in a positive way. Begin by accepting that you have an amazing body that deserves to be kept strong and healthy. Exercise regularly. Do something you enjoy, such as swimming, dancing or just going for a walk with your friends. Eating a healthy, balanced diet will give you energy, keep your body working well and help make you feel good about yourself. Try not to eat too much sugar but eat food that is tasty and good for a growing body. If you're worried about your weight, speak to your parents or see a doctor who can advise you on how to achieve a healthier weight if necessary.

Be proud

It's a waste of time and energy worrying about something you can't change, such as how tall or short you are. Start being proud of how strong and healthy your body is. If you spend a lot of time on your computer or watching TV, try and cut back and do something more active – once you start to move about you'll be surprised at how good it feels to run, walk, swim or play ball games in the park.

Sleep is important to **staying fit** and **feeling good**.
You need to get about 10 to 11 hours of sleep each night.

Eating disorders

Sometimes a negative body image can lead to eating disorders like anorexia and bulimia. If you are suffering from something like this speak to a trusted adult or phone a helpline (see page 31). There's no need to feel ashamed. No one will judge you, but you could be really damaging your health.

BEING BULLIED

Bullying can happen for lots of reasons but if you have low self-esteem you could be more of a target.

What is bullying?

People with low self-esteem are more likely to be bullied and cyberbullied because bullies are cowards and like to target people who are not assertive or confident. Bullying can be physical, such as pushing, hitting or pinching; emotional, such as being ignored in the playground and left out of social events; or verbal, such as being insulted, teased or ridiculed for any reason, including race, how you look and your gender.

Social media

Social media is a vital way of keeping in touch with friends, of knowing what's going on, who's doing what and what's in or out – you feel you have to stay online to be part of everything. This makes it easy for people to bully someone on social media. The bullies don't have to face their victim and they can get support by asking for 'likes' or sharing. This makes the bully feel more powerful and the victim feel more powerless. Cyberbullying is horrible and cowardly.

Here are ways to beat the cyberbullies...

Look for clubs or groups you can join or start a new hobby – this will distract you from what's happening online and will give you a chance to make new friends.

Block messages from cyberbullies and delete them without reading them. If you're going to report the cyberbullying, keep the messages as proof and ask an adult to check them out for you.

Take a digital detox. Switch off, even if it's only for a couple of hours in the evening when you get home.

Whatever is being said, you've no need to feel ashamed or embarrassed. The bullies are the ones who should be ashamed.

's hard, but try not to spond to cyberbullies his is what they want. Don't let them win.

itch your phone off at ght – don't lie awake aiting for nasty texts or tweets.

Cyberbullying

Cyberbullying is anything hurtful, abusive and offensive that is posted about you on digital media, such as Facebook, Twitter and Snapchat. It can be photos or text. It can also be when friends suddenly refuse to 'like' you or stop being 'friends' with you. Cyberbullying can happen at home, in school, every day and through the night. It's difficult to escape and it's one of the worst forms of bullying.

Talk to someone – a friend, teacher, family member… or phone a helpline (see page 31).

Are you a bully?

One of the reasons why a person becomes a bully can be because of their own low self-esteem and the need to feel better about themselves.

Why do people bully?

People become bullies for many different reasons – some because they have high self-esteem and feel they have the right to do what they like, others because they are bullied themselves at home, and some because they have low self-esteem and bullying others makes them feel better about themselves. Bullying is about having power and control over a situation or a person by whatever means necessary.

Silent bullying

Bullying is not always about physically hurting someone, it can be more subtle than that. Ignoring people, leaving them out of online chats, making a person believe he or she is not good enough to be part of the group, or starting false rumours and encouraging others to do the same are all ways to humiliate and belittle someone. Like all other forms of bullying this makes the person being bullied feel isolated and scared and can have very harmful results, such as depression and self-harming, while it makes the bully feel that they are pulling all the strings.

Stop being a bully

If you recognise yourself as being a bully, ask yourself why you do it. Is it because your own self-esteem is low, or maybe you're being bullied at home? Think about the consequences of bullying. It can make people feel ashamed and worthless and may even cause them to think about suicide. Do you really want to be the person who causes this kind of suffering?

Stop being bullied

Bullying is not the norm. It is not something that is part of growing up or that you have to laugh along with. No form of bullying should be tolerated – at home, in school or online. If your friends, family or peers tease you or joke about the way you look to your face or online, this is bullying and you do not have to put up with it. If you are being bullied or cyberbullied it's important that you tell a trusted adult, the police or phone a helpline.

BEING SHY

Lots of young people and adults are shy and most people feel shy at some point in certain situations.

What is being shy?

Shy people don't like to be the centre of attention and feel anxious about expressing their feelings or giving their own opinions, especially in a group. Surprisingly, many famous people, especially actors and comedians, say that they are shy and that they hide their shyness behind the roles they play. Most people feel shy when they start a new school, join a new club or group and have to make new friends. Remember that in these circumstances lots of other people will also be feeling shy and worried about the impression they're making.

Why shy?

Some people are born with a natural shyness or have become shy because they've been ridiculed, bullied or teased as a child. People who are shy often have lower self-esteem than talkative, outgoing people, and have trouble asserting themselves and getting or doing what they really want. They feel that everyone is looking at them and being critical, but the truth is they are probably their own worst critics.

Shy or introverted?

Introverts are people who are naturally quiet and prefer to be by themselves or to spend time with a best friend rather than in a big party of mates. Introverts may not be shy – they are quite happy to talk to a room full of people but they will want to go straight home afterwards rather than have to meet everyone at a party.

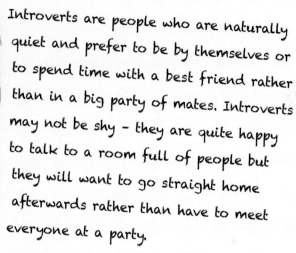

It's true, I used to be so shy. I used to never talk, just sit back and do my thing. I was never bullied, though, and it was never like it was something that needed to be 'fixed', like being shy is a bad thing.

Kendall Jenner (b. 1995), US model and TV personality

How to cope

There is nothing wrong with being shy as long as it doesn't stop you doing what you want to do. The world needs quiet and thoughtful people as well as loud, outgoing people. Shy people have their own special qualities, but if your shyness is stopping you from achieving what you want to, speak to someone you trust or phone a helpline, and check out pages 24–25 for ways to increase your confidence.

Being self-confident

Self-esteem and self-confidence are very similar and are often confused, but there is a difference.

What is self-confidence?

Self-esteem is about how you feel about yourself, whereas self-confidence is how you feel about your *abilities* to achieve something, be it a sport, exam, dance routine or new language. Some people have a healthy self-esteem but low self-confidence about some things, such as being able to write or do maths or play sports. Some people have low self-confidence when it comes to certain events or subjects, while others are negative about their abilities all the time.

Negative messages

A lack of self-confidence can start if you're constantly being told you can't do something. You may have a teacher who is always telling you that you're bad at science or will never do well in English. Or a friend who says you're useless at football or dancing … after a while you begin to believe all these negative messages and give up trying. If an adult is constantly putting you down, explain to them how it is affecting your self-confidence and discuss some of the positive things you can do to improve your ability in that particular subject.

If your friends tease you or criticise you all the time, tell them how you feel. If they carry on, maybe it's time to get some new friends who will encourage and support you.

TALKBACK!

What is the best way to support a friend who has low self-confidence?

Tell them how great they are and that they can do anything if they try hard enough.

Help them realise that failing is not a bad thing and that you'll be there for them no matter what happens.

PRESSURE...

It can be tough being a young person these days. There's school, friends, exams and family to cope with, and that's not all ...

High expectations

Pre-teens and teens are often under a lot of pressure – you're expected to look good, study hard and pass loads of tests and exams, be popular and have lots of mates, and all at a time when you're changing physically and emotionally and trying to find your place in the world.

> *Peer pressure* to be cool, **fit in** and **be one of the crowd** is also strong at this age.

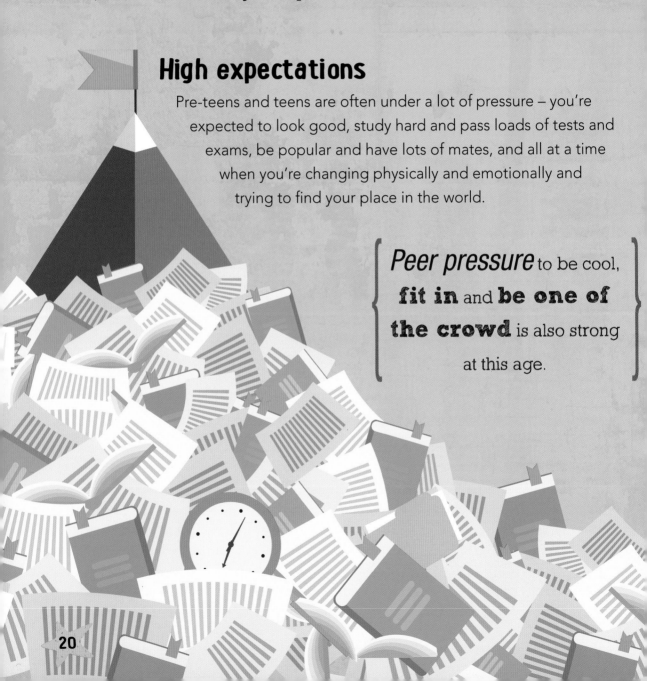

Your future

School is important. Getting a good education means you have a better chance of getting the sort of job you want and having an enjoyable and fulfilling career. Decide what you want to do and what you want out of life; don't be influenced by what your friends or siblings are doing. Discuss your plans with your family, a teacher or close friend who will encourage and support you. Don't let poor self-esteem or a lack of confidence stop you from achieving what you want to do at school. If you feel unsure about your abilities, talk to a teacher. There may be more options than you think.

Social pressures

Schoolwork aside, there is often pressure from friends and peers to look a certain way, to socialise and to join in. Everyone seems to have busy lives, loads of friends and lots of things to do. For people with low self-esteem this can be very challenging. You may just want to sit quietly and read, or watch a film by yourself, or have a quiet time with your best mate. This is your choice, so be polite but say 'no' to invitations if they are not right for you – real friends will respect your decision. A few best friends who appreciate you for who you really are can be worth more than lots of mates who want you to be like them.

Being assertive

Being assertive is being able to voice your opinion, ask for what you want and disagree without being disrespectful.

Can't say no

People with low self-esteem and who lack confidence can find it difficult to say 'no' even to something they really don't want to do or strongly disagree with. For them it's easier to say 'yes' and go along with everyone else than step out of line and risk being shunned for not wanting to do what everyone else wants. People with low self-esteem might also find it difficult to suggest things to do in case their mates think their ideas are silly, but why should they?

No thanks. I'm going home to read.

Sorry. I can't. I told Mum I'd be home for tea.

Does anyone want to see that new film?

Football's not for me so I'll see you tomorrow.

What is being assertive?

Being assertive means being able to express your opinion and ask for what you want in a positive, friendly way and being able to disagree with someone without being aggressive or nasty. Being assertive is not the same as being aggressive or always wanting to get your own way. It's respecting your own thoughts and wishes as well as those of others, even if they are not the same as yours.

Peer pressure

People who lack assertiveness are far more likely to give in to peer pressure. They want to please everyone and are afraid of losing friends so they say 'yes' to things their friends and classmates suggest even if those things might upset them or get them into trouble. Lacking assertiveness is a bit of a vicious circle – the more you agree to things you don't want to do, the less self-respect you have, and the more likely you are to lack assertiveness. Talk to a friend or adult you can trust about how you feel. By building up your self-confidence and self-esteem (see page 24) you will be able to be more assertive and tackle peer pressure and do the things you want to do, not what others want you to do.

TALKBACK!

Do you think being assertive is really that important?

I don't see what's wrong with going along with what everyone else wants to do. Why rock the boat?

It's good to join in with everyone else but sometimes you need to say what you want and others should fit in with you.

CONFIDENCE BOOSTERS!

Try these tips and techniques to help increase your self-esteem and boost your self-confidence and assertiveness.

Up your self-esteem

✓ Think about a time when you felt happy and confident and really proud of yourself. Remember how good you felt. Tap into these positive thoughts when you feel down or stressed.

✓ Make a list of the things you can do well – anything from singing or dancing, playing a sport, spelling or doing card tricks. Try and practise your skills every day and get better at them.

✓ Think of all the kind, helpful things you do every day – chores at home, visiting your grandparents, listening to your best friend's troubles. Appreciate what a special person you are, not only to yourself but also to other people.

✓ Instead of saying 'I can't' say 'I can... I'll give it a try'. And try something new – even if it's something small. And when you've achieved something new, give yourself a high-five and smile!

… to negative thoughts about yourself. When you hear those negative messages saying you're not good enough, too stupid or can't do it, imagine a big boot kicking them out of your mind or stamping them into the ground. You've got better things to think about!

SAY YES!

… to positive images of yourself. Visualise yourself as happy and healthy and doing the things you want to do really well – playing football, learning how to swim, knitting a scarf or reading that big novel at long last. Picture how proud you are of yourself.

How to be more assertive

- Take some time to think about how you feel and what you want. Notice how many times you say 'yes' when you mean 'no', or say that you 'don't care' or 'don't mind' when you do.

- Next time a friend asks you to go somewhere or do something, think for a few seconds and then answer truthfully – say 'no' if you want to, but be polite. If it helps, make an excuse that you have homework to do, or are expected at home. By starting to respect what you want to do, you will build up your self-esteem.

- Practise saying 'I' as in 'I would like to do this', or 'I prefer', even if it's only in front of the mirror or to your pet! Sounds silly, but you may not have heard yourself say that for a long time.

- Believe that your opinions and ideas are as good and as important as anyone else's.

- Suggest something that you and your best mate or friends can do together. even if it's just going to see a film or going bowling – be the one to take the initiative.

Learning difficulties

People with learning difficulties face bigger challenges than most and this can make them stronger.

What are learning difficulties?

Learning difficulties are quite common and mean that for some people it is harder to learn certain things, such as writing, reading and maths. Anyone can have learning difficulties. No one really knows why some people have them and others don't, but they can be genetic; that is, passed down through the family.

> People with learning difficulties are not slow or stupid. They just **learn** things in a *different* way.

Feeling stupid

Children often don't realise that they have a problem when they first start to learn, and many begin to feel angry and frustrated because they don't grasp things as quickly or easily as their classmates. It might feel like trying to do a jigsaw with some of the pieces missing. They can feel slow and stupid and this can lead to low self-esteem. Once a child has a learning difficulty diagnosed, the teachers and family can begin to tackle the issues with the child and build up confidence.

No obstacles

Many successful and famous people have had learning difficulties and have become hugely successful and achieved their dreams. It may take a lot of effort and extra hard work, but there is nothing to stop those with a learning problem achieving anything they put their mind to. In fact, as they may have to work harder than their classmates they should feel extra proud of themselves.

Just as good

People with learning difficulties deserve the same respect as anyone else, and they should not allow themselves to be bullied or made to feel useless by their family, friends or schoolmates. If you're being bullied, or you see someone with learning difficulties being bullied who cannot stand up for themselves, report it to a teacher. If you think it's serious, tell the police.

Physical disabilities

Having a physical disability can make you feel isolated and vulnerable. But it shouldn't stop you from trying to achieve your goals. Look for groups and clubs that have the facilities for your disability. Speak to your teachers or doctor about therapies that can help you. There will always be those who will tease you, but try to ignore them. Suggest to your teacher that you give a talk to assembly or the class about your disability so that others understand what it is and how it affects you. Report bullying to a teacher or trusted adult. You have the right to feel as safe and be as confident as anyone else.

SO, TO RECAP...

This is a recap of the issues we've looked at in this book. They are presented as ideas to discuss. Talking things through can help us to understand ourselves a little better and why we feel the way we do in certain situations.

Why is self-esteem important?

If we feel good about ourselves we have a healthy or high self-esteem. If we feel useless or worthless, this means our self-esteem is bad, or low. Why is it important to have a healthy self-esteem? How can we get a healthy self-esteem? Can we get a healthy self-esteem by ourselves or do we need the approval of others?

Building a better body image

It's very easy to become obsessed about how we look. Why do you think this is? Is it the same for boys and girls? How can we build a better body image? Getting fit and eating a healthy diet are ways to help us feel better about ourselves. Why do you think this is?

Accept who you are

Part of having a healthy self-esteem is to think about our own special talents and what it is that makes you unique. What does it mean to accept who you are? Should we try to b like other people? What are some reasons why v might not like ourselves?

Being shy – no big deal

Being shy is not a bad thing. Some people are shy most of the time, others when they're in a new situation or meeting people for the first time. Most people feel shy at some time. Can you remember a time when you felt shy? Why do you think it's good to have some people who are shy and some people who aren't?

I can do it!

Many of us are self-confident about most things, but may be unsure when it comes to trying something new. Sometimes our self-confidence takes a knock when we are given a lot of negative messages from others saying we're no good at certain things. How do you think you can get over a lack of confidence? How can you support a friend or sibling who lacks confidence?

Say no!

Often we can find ourselves doing things to please others even if we know they're not right or we shouldn't be doing them. Or we might think that what we want to do is boring or silly, so we don't mention it. This is when you need to be more assertive. Can you think of a time when you needed to be more assertive? What would you do differently if it happened again? Why do you think some people are more assertive than others?

Glossary

adolescence a period after puberty (about 8–16 years of age) when a person develops physically from a child into an adult

anorexia an eating disorder when the person stops eating or eats very little to lose weight

anxious feeling worried or nervous about how something is going to turn out

ashamed feeling embarrassed about not having done something well enough or about the way you look or behave

assertive being confident; having the ability to express your own opinions and wants in a way that is not aggressive

balanced diet a healthy diet that includes the right amount from the five food groups including five portions of fruit and vegetables

body image how you see yourself; your idea of how your body looks or how it should look

bulimia an eating disorder that involves binging or overeating and then getting sick or starving to keep weight low

depression feeling unhappy and without hope

facilities equipment and space for a particular purpose, such as a gym, disabled toilets and wheelchair access

gender male, female or transgender (when a person changes their gender)

genetic biological characteristics that are inherited from one person to another through family genes

hormones chemical substances that move around the body and help to keep it working properly

humiliate make someone feel stupid or foolish by making them look silly in front of other people

inferior feeling not as good as other people

initiative acting or taking charge before others do

learning difficulties having problems learning everyday things or new skills

low self-esteem feeling that you are not good enough, that you can't do things properly

obsessive thinking or worrying about a certain thing all the time

peer pressure when you feel you have to do something you don't want to because your friends or classmates are doing it

peers people of your own age such as classmates and friends

race a group of people linked by the way they look or where they come from

ridiculed being made to look silly; laughed at

self-belief believing that you can do something and that you are good enough to achieve what you want to

self-confidence the belief that you can achieve something or are good at doing things

self-doubt not sure that you can achieve what you want to; doubting your own abilities

self-esteem the way you feel about yourself and your abilities to achieve things

sibling brother or sister

therapies treatments that can help to heal or improve a physical or mental condition

under-achiever someone who doesn't perform as well or achieve as much as they can

unworthy feeling that you do not deserve success or the respect of others

Further information

Note to parents and teachers: every effort has been made by the Publishers to ensure that websites are suitable for children, that they are of the highest educational value, and that they contain no inappropriate or offensive material. However, because of the nature of the Internet, it is impossible to guarantee that the contents of these sites will not be altered. We strongly advise that Internet access is supervised by a responsible adult.

WEBSITES AND HELPLINES

If you feel overwhelmed by any of the issues you've read about in this book or need advice, check out a website or call a helpline and talk to someone who will understand.

www.brainline.org/content/2009/05/who-me-self-esteem-for-people-with-disabilities.html
How to boost self-esteem regardless of disabilities.

www.gosh.nhs.uk/children/general-health-advice/eat-smart/food-science/improving-your-diet
A look at the food groups and tips on how to eat a better, healthier diet.

http://kidshealth.org/en/kids/shy.html
What it means to be shy; how to help yourself or a friend who is shy if it is affecting how they behave.

www.themix.org.uk
A site for young people to get advice on a range of issues including emotions, sex and learning difficulties. Discussion boards, chat line.

www.take-your-power.com/how-build-self-confidence.html
Advice on how to build your self-confidence in small and big ways.

www.childline.org.uk
Find out about issues that are troubling you, meet others, message or call the 24-hour helpline for advice or someone who'll just listen.
Helpline: 0800 1111.

www.youngminds.org.uk
Information and advice for children and young people experiencing bullying, stress and mental or emotional anxieties.

www.samaritans.org
Advice and support for anyone in distress. The helpline is 08457 90 90 90.

www.sane.org/get-help
Online and phone help for mental and emotional issues with a dedicated helpline for young people.

www.supportline.org.uk
A charity giving emotional support to children and young people.

For readers in Australia and New Zealand

www.healthdirect.gov.au/partners/kids-helpline
A helpline for young people giving advice, counselling and support.

https://kidshelpline.com.au
Online and phone help for a wide range of issues.

www.kidsline.org.nz
Helpline run by specially trained young volunteers to help kids and teens deal with troubling issues and problems.

Index

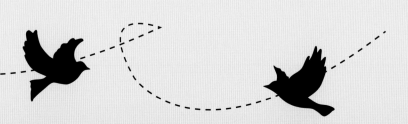

Fear of Failure

What is a fear of failure? • No one is born with a fear of failure • Making mistakes • Do you have a fear of failure? • High expectations • School stress • Friends for ever? • Self-esteem and failure • Make failure a success • Be inspired • What is *your* success? • Overcoming your fear

Cultural Issues

What is culture? • Culture and religion • Culture and law • A changing society • Stereotyping • Old v new • Clashes at home • Your rights matter • I am what I wear • Prejudice and discrimination • Dealing with prejudice • Respect!

Family Differences

A family today • Fighting families • Divorce • Single parent family • Trust and abuse • Manage your anger • Problems with siblings • Child carers • Living on the breadline • My life! • Family breakdown • Foster and adoption • Illness and death

Self-esteem and Confidence

What is self-esteem? • Body image • A healthy body image • You are unique • Being shy • What is self-confidence? • Pressure! • Being assertive • Learning difficulties • Bullied or bully?

Understanding Sexuality

Time for change • What is sexuality? • Being lesbian, gay or bisexual • Where do I fit in? • Setting the record straight • Coming out • Homophobia – it's not right • Dealing with bad feelings • Being accepted • Proud to be me!

Understanding Transgender

What is gender? • What is transgender? • Transgender is not LGB • The real me • Family support • School policy • Bullying and discrimination • Puberty – help! • Be inspired • Transitioning – the journey • Your true self